A TOURIST IN LUDLOW

and Other Poems

❧

POETRY & WATERCOLORS
by Charles E. Wadsworth

THE TIDAL PRESS
1984

ACKNOWLEDGEMENTS

I am beholden to Christopher Fry and Leslie Norris, both of whom read the poems in manuscript, bringing to their readings perception and charity. Both, quite independently, arrived at a similar injunction. They reminded me that concision can be more persuasive than effusion. Although I tried to give full weight to their admonitions, I am aware that if I had retained only the leanest lines and those potentially immortal I would have been left with the slimmest of slim volumes.

In the course of my endless revisions, my wife Jeannie reminded me that the seventeenth alteration may not eliminate all the flaws left over from the sixteenth. She assured me, when I despaired of immaculate perfection, that imperfection is a widespread, inescapable human characteristic, prevalent among poets, painters, peasants and husbands, adding that we must all go out into the world with our sins and wens upon us. So be it. We do, not what we would do, but what we can.

❧

❧

LCC 83-72233   ISBN—0—930954—19—x

The Tidal Press : Cranberry Isles : Maine 04625

*For
my wife
Jeannie, who
both assisted
and insisted*

I first thought to call this book 'The Return Of The Native' but that would be poaching on the territory of a very fine poet indeed. The shade of Thomas Hardy would have cause to reproach me. Then, too, that title would have been misleading. Even though, during my first English sojourn and on subsequent visits, I often experienced a kind of homecoming sensation — a curious blend of the familiar and the foreign — a born and bred American can, at best, qualify as a native Englishman only by empathy.

I had first encountered the lilting pessimisms of A. E. Housman as a youth. There is something in Housman's singing despair that appeals peculiarly to the dolors of adolescence. But more than that, his bittersweet quatrains had stimulated me to the explorations of the wide and various delights other poets had to offer. It seemed, therefore, appropriate that my first purpose during that first English sojourn was to pay pilgrim tribute to Housman by visiting Ludlow where his ashes were buried. It seemed equally appropriate that that visit should have suggested the title of 'A Tourist In Ludlow' for this book.

I wanted also, on that first trip to England, to see as many original Turner watercolors as were seeable, since I knew them, for the most part, only in reproduction. It was the excitement of that encounter with a number of his radiant watercolors that spurred me to the use of that elusive, fascinating and often frustrating medium as an accompaniment to the poems in this book, all of which were begun in the tiny village of East Dean, Sussex — and most of which were revised and finished in retrospect on the equally small, floating township called Cranberry Isles, Maine.

CHARLES E. WADSWORTH
Cranberry Isles, Maine
1983

CONTENTS

A TOURIST IN LUDLOW

and Other Poems

A TOURIST IN LUDLOW

1.

The parish church of Ludlow stands
Where Tudor houses, black and white,
Remind the church that it demands
Partitioning of wrong from right.

But I to Ludlow came that day,
Twentieth century born and bred,
Doubting what Man or God might say,
Drawn to a poet's final bed.

I felt that I was in his debt
For gifts he hadn't known he gave,
Yet gifts I'd rather not forget
And would remember at his grave.

From his verse I was first to learn
That cold print, formal on a page,
Could be preserving flame and burn
Permanently with love and rage.

His words all fled from voiceless clay,
His ashes now a pulseless fire,
What would I find of him that day,
In Shropshire—or in any shire?

2.

Then, past the open gate, I saw
Among the dying autumn beds,
Tidying up the natural law,
Clipping the shaggy, seed-rich heads,

An old sexton, who chanced to look
At me, leaned on his clotted spade,
And said, pointing at my guide-book,
"These are the fields where roses fade."

15

He chuckled. "It's just there ahead,
If Housman's is the grave you search,
Or if Ambrosia's instead,
She lies there snug within the church."

He paused and lopped a raveled rose.
"Can't say his leavings helped the loam.
Few of the locals here propose
Shropshire had ever been his home.

None knows for sure; I'd guess, perhaps,
The land he talked of never was,
A place you couldn't draw on maps,
'Though some might say he did and does.

Someone planted a cherry tree.
Seemed the proper thing to try it.
Did less than nothing; died you see.
Couldn't stand a Housman diet."

Sextons, like Gods, must have their joke;
I smiled, acknowledging his jest,
Though wondered if those quiet folk,
The churchyard dead, laughed last and best.

Garrulous, he resumed his talk,
A guide and critic rolled in one,
And pointed down the graveled walk.
"You know, when all is said and done,

It must be lonely where he's lain.
They might have found a place inside;
Naught's cold as ashes soaked with rain.
They say he came back here to hide."

Girded in stark and stoic pride,
Never a man the fool of hope,
Had he believed a man *could* hide,
Or quite elude the hangman's rope?

And yet, despite that tragic mood,
In verse as light as bitter-sweet,
Composing with notes men have rued,
He shaped his songs from man's defeat.

Refreshing as astringent wine,
They linger on our tongue awhile.
Cleansing our palate, they refine
A taste for too sweet lines and style.

4.

The old man thanked, I walked along
And stopped beside a simple plaque.
An English robin, hard at song,
Practiced nearby the singer's knack.

A smaller robin, strange to me,
Subject of a smaller nation,
He made his modest poetry,
True as a bard to his vocation.

There Housman's ashes quiet lie,
Buried beneath the northern wall,
Where busy tourists passing by
May never see his grave at all.

And tourist I, a thing of mirth,
As all such are who roam and range,
Unlocal anywhere on earth,
My accent wrong, my clothing strange,

Greeted a fellow tourist where,
Lodged in his voiceless hostelry,
Deaf to the sound of verse or prayer
Or praise, he toured eternity.

5.

Singer who found this life a curse,
Redeemable by death at best,
Though mitigated some by verse,
Have you a home at last and rest?

Or, restless though you sleep alone,
A stranger still, your ghost unlaid,
Do you recall that flesh and bone
Which sheltered you in towered shade?

Now, townsman of that stillest town,
Unwarmed by either love or hate,
Cold to rejection or renown,
Sleep is your garment, soon or late.

Since sleep is what you wanted most
You have no reason to complain;
No holy or unholy ghost
Brings you now either dreams or pain.

6.

Should you rise some Shropshire morning,
I'm not sure you'd find things better;
Hard upon the moment's borning
Man's still bound by breath's light fetter.

Though things have changed a bit since you,
Strolling the castle-shadowed ways,
Brooded on lovers, false and true,
Man's destinies and tangled days.

Spewing their fumes on country airs,
Cyclists like spastic wasps replace,
Where once the yeomen cried their wares,
The chaffer of the market-place.

Where once the gibbet swung its crop
—Bleak harvest of brutality—
A pylon crowns that same hill-top
With more benign geometry.

Benign we're told yet not quite yet
Do earth's foundations steady lie.
Though fashions change in daily fret,
Trouble is still in good supply.

Everything's still the same yet changed,
Some angels topple still from grace
And good-and-ill though rearranged
Visages forth the world's same face.

Now as then the coins we cherish
Aren't those the sun on flowers spilt,
Fool's gold that at dusk will perish,
But that we sweat from rock and silt.

7.

Today, when lads row on the Teme,
It's not quatrains they have in mind,
But some hydroelectric scheme
That's bound to put the Teme in bind.

Lads in the village pubs debate
—Voices near drowned in telly sound—
Their fortunes in a welfare state,
Foundering on the sinking pound.

We, craning at Man's satellites,
That brand brief orbits on the dark,
May fail to note in star-shot heights,
Brands that outlast Man's every spark.

Since earth and space we mold and rend,
Who's to tell us and God apart?
There's little we can't make or mend,
Unless, perhaps, a broken heart.

We have forgotten what the Greeks
Once knew. Hubris still claims its fee
And we who stride on mountain peaks
Risk terminal catastrophe.

Nothing has changed that much I think;
The soulless sell their souls for fame,
The brew's no sweeter that we drink,
The cards still stacked in every game.

The coin's dull clink sounds of alloy,
And bears a remnant, ravaged face.
We ransom kings to buy a toy,
We all still lose the longest race.

And men still slay as enemies
Those they would just as soon were friends,
Obeying far diplomacies
That twist their wills toward bloody ends.

8.

Would you then broach a grand design,
Postulate, say, some social plan?
Or would you suggest men resign
Themselves, within their turmoiled span

To brevity, their lives and doom
Unnoticed by the careless dark,
Like transients in a hired room
Who leave behind no lasting mark.

Perhaps, though truths of poetry
Are truths we did not know we'd known,
Couched as immortal novelty,
A passing permanence on loan.

"Tourist in Ludlow," you might say,
"Search otherwhere; expect from me
No final cure for man's dismay.
Death *may* be life's sole remedy.

I offer here no key or clue,
Since, after all, there may be none,
Or weren't, at least, for lads I knew,
Stricken beneath a stricken sun.

Travel on tourist; ask no more:
The dead have earned their right to hide
From all who'd question or implore.
There *is* no truth I can provide

Save this: Those who would walk upright
When lightnings vein the thundered air,
With shattered fragments of their fright
Must build a song against despair."

PETWORTH DAFFODILS

Through Petworth House, where paintings climb the walls,
And Gibbon's chiseled virtuosities
Abound, we strolled, but nothing seemed to please,
And realized, in Spring, art sometimes palls.

No amount of Turners may then fulfill
Our needs, no masterpiece may satisfy,
No Hals or Rembrandt can then hope to vie
With Spring, which, glimpsed through windows, worked its will.

So out we fled, to wander Petworth Park,
Through sunshot breezes with an April bite,
Past a magnolia, uncurling tight
Blooms, toward a grove of great beeches whose dark

Dignities were lightened by fledgling green;
Then spied where turf verged into unshorn slopes,
Like small trumpets fanfaring summer hopes,
The first host of wild daffodils we'd seen;

Wordsworth's once, but now, that moment ours,
Living daffodils held in living eyes,
Affirming we must not outgrow surprise,
Or ever become immune to flowers.

Though if we'd happened not to pass that way,
Not one furled pregnancy of petaled gold
Would one less fluted filigree unfold,
Nor one less blossom its pressing purpose stay.

There, in the flinty, chalk-dank soil, silent
As growth, they'd pursued their vegetable plans,
Their stratagems of increase old as man's,
In their speechless patience, more eloquent.

Now, in April incitement, their long rest
Stirred by the tilting earth to urgencies,
In a bright cause that leaves no casualties,
They'd stormed one small knoll in golden conquest.

No landscape architect's flowering dream;
Native to the uncurried bank or down;
Unsanctioned by Capability Brown;
They'd bloomed, adherents of a wilder scheme.

No artist who's been or will ever be,
Out of the sourest or the sweetest soil,
Could or will, with so little sense of toil
Or strain, mine pure gold so instinctively.

THE DUCKS OF EAST DEAN

It's not bad being a mallard duck in East Dean,
In a small pond,
In the middle of a small round green,
Where you can keep a shiny eye on the passing scene.

Where all the citizenry, foolish and fond,
Stop to distribute bread,
And an occasional tidbit or biscuit.
You don't have to worry about getting ahead;
You don't have to suffer or lack.
As for the rounder world—why risk it?—
When all it takes is a quack
Or two to get a meal,
Where water and troubles roll off your back;
Where, should your feet get too wet, you can afford
To spend some time drying them on thick English sward.
Yours is a small round world but it has appeal.

It's not bad being a mallard duck in East Dean.
If you carry a piece of the sky on each wing,
Or your head is a rainbow-delectable green,
You don't have to envy the way thrushes sing.

I've known a few worlds, some here, some there,
I would say it is true of worlds anywhere;
You don't have to worry, you don't have to care,
If you're buoyant and rounded with a pert derrière.
I know, I know it's so.
The
     fairest
         world
             is
                 not
                    quite
                       fair!

A CAST OF THOUSANDS

FOR NELL HAMPTON

A cast of thousands, drawn in full detail,
The living mingling freely with the dead,
Throng compatibly, dear Nell, through your head,
On call to populate your every tale.
Listening I grow confused. Being time's
Drudge—unlike you or them—I cannot tell
Which greet me in village lanes and which dwell
Speechlessly beneath churchyard yews and limes.

But you, convinced all should be included,
The saved, the lost, the sober and the droll,
Provide everyone with a speaking role;
On your ample stage none is excluded.

In scenes you set, your village cast, and me,
Play out our parts—as long as yours shall be.

CANTERBURY CATHEDRAL

Lapsed Christians, our worn parcels of frayed creed
Bulk small next to your scarred and faith-warmed flanks.
You exact from us shame-faced, pilgrim thanks,
Where, in the shadow of the faith-wrought deed,
Our eyes spire upward. An arched asylum
Waits within. There, pleasant ladies dispense
For restoration funds, at twenty pence,
Brochures that feature Becket's martyrdom.

Asylum, it would seem, exists nowhere,
And yet the wingéd arches still attest,
They, like our hope of heaven, will not rest;
Their reaching nearly permanent as prayer.

Enlightened past faith, here we can't but sense
In these grave stones a weightless radiance.

This is no hallowed site where pilgrims came;
No student of the faith or its stone shapes,
In cathedrals where mystery is defined
And made manifest, is ever inclined
To stop by. Half lost in billowed landscapes,
It must be sought. Once found, it makes small claim.

Here no roll-call of grandeur can be heard.
Canterbury, Lincoln, York and Ely,
Durham, Salisbury, Winchester and Wells,
Whose high holiness, in crescendo, swells
Across time, fall mute. Here there is only
The sound of a small breeze and smaller bird.

Within no faith-stained windows blaze as aids
To zeal, yet this squat space, more white-washed cave
Than church, which brings most to mind a stable,
Seems as fit a place to stage that fable
Or fact which raised it as the tallest nave
In all the land. Quietly it persuades.

If the old tale is true many have told,
This haven sheltered by a surging down,
And twice sheltered by an ancient yew-tree,
Whose shepherd flock in turn sheltered newly
Born lambs and torn ewes, best recalls the renown
Of shepherds a great light struck dumb and gold.

A myth perhaps, though some have held it true.
Acts of belief, down centuries accrued,
Which generations spent on buttressed spires
And walls to hold aloft faith's fortress fires,
Sprang from a cornerstone as stable-rude
As this chapel—and small as a seed of yew.

AN ENGLISHMAN'S GARDEN

A garden is something an Englishman,
Truly English, would no more do without
Than a Bishop would preach an Easter sermon
Clad only in God's love and a breech-clout.
In every class and accent it's agreed
That gardens are a fundamental need.

Those cosseted, tended, splendid borders
Wherein each specimen is prime and prize
And dociled to head gardener's orders,
Come as no revelation or surprise.
About "great houses," riding swells of turf,
They foam and break in well-bred, blossomed surf.

Big Ben's toll behind them, commuters flee
London's toil for suburban Surbiton,
Eager for that rural facsimile
Gardens provide near villas hardly won,
In latter-day Andrew Marvell bowers
Where marvellous "green shades" dapple flowers.

And should it be "quaint cots" you have in mind
—"Rose-smothered," "bee-drowsy" and "rushy-thatched"—
I don't know where you could expect to find
That yeoman-simple, herbal charm is matched.
Strangers in our time, yet they still ensure
A few flowered follies briefly endure.

But London's grim hem, where homes of mean grief
And scant hopes clot, puts on the bravest show.
A small plot, soiled as a used handkerchief,
Glimpsed from a train, will flaunt a scarlet glow
Where expectations are dimmer, God knows,
Than that flame from a single, "standard" rose.

SUSSEX BLUEBELLS

These bluebells have no purpose that I know,
Unless, that is, one chooses to construe
They instruct the sky in a deeper blue,
As heaven might learn love from earth below;
Not from those who, with fair heaven at stake,
Love only to accumulate credit,
But from those, heedless of gain or debit,
Who, now and then, love for love's own sweet sake.

I, for one, would not really want to choose
That tint the sky achieves by endlessness
Over the bluebell hue of rootedness,
When here, between the two, I have both blues;
Both mine, not selfishly to own or flaunt,
But because each serves a separate want.

THE LEAF-WALKER

The boxwood hedge, with twigs and leaves grown dense,
Now acts as both a boundary and a fence,
So any wind that pelts against its side
Hardly disturbs the lives concealed inside.

If any nests or nestlings are within,
They're safe from every brusque and windy din.
So thick's the fretted structure and its eaves,
That when the mother bustles in or leaves,
You wonder how she'd ever have an eye
For where her small, ravenous young-ones lie.

I watch her flirt along the leveled top,
And then, as though upon a signal, stop,
Cock her head, hesitate, then skip a pace
Or two, till satisfied she's found her place.

Though feather-light, somehow it does seem strange
She can walk the hedge and not disarrange
That stream of overlapping, seamless green,
Then quickly seem to sink within, unseen,
As might a rabbit vanish in a hat
Which had no openings for a trick like that.

So slick she flicks, so deftly disappears,
That to the wondering watcher she appears
A water-walker sinking toward her brood
Through chinks of faith—each drowning love renewed.

THE WIDOW

The days may work counter to what we are;
We, in the end, may be what we are not.
While she'd been born beneath a lavish star,
Her husband lived for getting, getting, got,
And she, infected by his avarice,
For love diminishing herself to him,
Took on a cupidity great as his,
Her generosity a star grown dim.

As any bee knows how to make honey,
So another knack is widely known.
Few have trouble learning to spend money.
Him dead, it was for her a skill outgrown.

All those days, months, years as a miser's wife,
And she'd forgot how to make or spend her life.

SUSSEX CLAY

If God has any need of clay,
If he would like to try again
His minor art of making men,
I'd recommend that any day

In April when mists like sheep flock
Through almost any Sussex lane,
Near where farmsteads and meadows drain,
He'd find the clay in tidy stock.

Hard by the churchyard gate there's lots,
Near where the guarding gate hangs loose,
From clay that had a former use,
Escaping there from graveyard plots.

If he feels the primal vision
Stands now in need of major change,
Here it is easy to arrange
Brand-new clay for his revision.

In fact this grey, pervasive ore
Is somewhat more than he would need,
Unless his plan should quite exceed
His vastest plan planned heretofore.

There's a surfeit of sticky dough,
The sort a potter's hand might knead,
That feet of men and livestock breed
In daily traffic to and fro.

He needn't worry what it's worth;
He could be as prodigal as God.
This season finds the land well-trod
And churned, drenched with moisture, the earth

Nearly as liquid as the air.
If all that clay just meets God's need,
He'd best note a contending greed.
I saw yesterday, here and there,

Where quiet turf joins quiet clay,
Some spikes of green piercing the slough
With keener tines than fork or plow,
Clearly indicating that they

—Green soldiers without rank or name—
Had their invasion well in hand
And took that clay to be their land;
They had already staked a claim.

He, who had made both men and grass,
If now on man's revision bent,
Must settle for his first intent,
Accepting what had come to pass.

Now unavailable for men
Much of that clay was occupied.
Already something lived inside,
And God had better think again.

GLORIOUS GOODWOOD

FOR LESLIE NORRIS

There has never been a lovelier place,
There has never been a livelier scene
In which to watch high clouds and horses race;
One across the blue, one across the green,
Or silk-slick jockeys, wizened, wise and spry
Discuss with silken ladies the chances
Of their mounts, where fillies, mincing by
In the paddock perform skittish dances
Like female Pegasi who long to fly;

While I, a rail-bird at the paddock fence
—No customary perch for me at all—
With no idea, no wagerer's sense
Of form, drift as tidal odds rise and fall
And can't decide which system is for me,
And at last, proclaiming them all the same
Invent one rooted in poetry:
A filly's sleek beauty of frame and name,
Tainted but slightly with cupidity.

I ignored what a poet friend of mine
Had said, who'd studied well words and horses,
Who'd thrilled to the beats of a racing line
Of verse and hoof-beats at racing courses.
For bettors, he warned, no metaphor would serve;
A sober study of thoroughbred deeds
Was needed, their staying power and nerve
In past performances. Beautiful steeds
Could deceive by grooming and race-day verve.

Jubilant, Mallabee, Saint Rouge and Noor,
Shantanna and Hillbrow passed in review,
Then Pagan Queen, Pilley Green—them and more—
Till, spotting her glide by, I finally knew
She'd make a sure thing of my wagering,
She'd guarantee my pound its swiftest flight,
Multiplying it freely on the wing.
I couldn't lose with Lady Of The Night,
By Midsummer Night from Love Lies Bleeding.

That difficult decision finally made,
Both art and money riding on one steed,
Trying to forget how seldom art has paid,
Great with aesthetic rectitude and greed,
I turned toward where the centaurs that fine day
Would run, dazzled still by Lady's suave pride,
Her lance-tip ears, her wind-teased mane, the play
Of shimmering tremors across her hide,
Her wide, white-rimmed eyes, her high, tingling neigh,

And threaded my bemused path toward shrill ranks
Of bookies who, like berserk semaphores,
In a tongue known to them and racing cranks,
Flashed odds above the gadding crowds in lores
As ancient and inscrutable as death
Or life. Approaching one of them I drew
From my wallet one green pound Elizabeth
And The Bank Of England both said would do
For all transactions, and with bated breath,

—As though this were the first step down rambling,
Rosy paths, which in youth I'd been told led
To dread perils of compulsive gambling—
Spoke to the bored, black-clad bookie and said,
Mustering my raciest, rakish look,
"I'll lay a pound on Lady Of The Night."
And he, though unillusioned as a rook,
Raised one brow, like a rumpled bird in flight,
Shrugged, gave me a shoddy stub and marked his book.

"What are the odds you're quoting?" I inquired.
His face cracked widely in a sudden grin.
"Best odds since Agincourt—if she's inspired
That is. She's fifty to one, mate, to win."
And I, as though some oracle had let
Me in on a secret too sibylline
For his crass ears, winked, and, swaggering, set
Out toward a spot where the race might be seen,
Where, enjoying her triumph, I would get

The best view of Lady, my flying horse.
There she, swifter than swallows or the fall
Of losing tickets round green Goodwood's course,
Would set a pace guaranteed to appall
Such entries as had the effrontery
To challenge her, they, less filly than mare,
More like dowagers strolling before tea
Than like Lady—arch-prowed, wind-fleet corsair—
Whose hoofs would beat the beat of poetry.

And then—"They're off."—I heard the stirring shout
And the far milling at the starting gate
Became a faint frieze, mount and man without
Distinction, a single, multi-hooved, great
Equine surge. Lady would need more than pluck
(Twenty-two entries is more a stampede
Than a race.) not to be left in the ruck.
No jockey named, not Piggott pedigreed,
I prayed the unknown jockey's name was Luck.

Drumming the lush and lilting turf, around
The first bend they swept, strung out now into
Separate horses, separate men while the sound
Of pounding hooves and pounding pulses grew
And the yips of backers pelted the air
Until they passed me, straining toward the post;
A blur of the clown-bright hues jockeys wear,
Of fetlocks, forelocks, haunches, hocks, a host
Of kaleidoscopic shapes—but nowhere,

Nowhere, the slightest sign of Lady's fate
Or figure while I stood there stunned and dumb.
Had she been left there grazing at the gate
Or gazing at the sky, where cloud shapes come
And go, while other fillies no fleeter
Than she in that aristocratic mob
Of mounts, unconcerned with rhyme or meter,
Had leapt forward, their poetry their job?
I waited, disconsolate, to greet her.

I waited but she never hove in sight,
Then tore the mocking stub of our defeat.
The warnings about gambling had been right
And Lady's beauty nothing but deceit.
"Don't judge the taste of a peach by its fuzz."
And such-like saws I recalled being told.
"Beauty's not what it seems but what it does."
And "Don't bet on a horse the day it's foaled."
But, oh my God, how beautiful she was.

Brooding on my small folly, not my worst,
I sauntered sobered from the dwindling scene,
One pound lighter than I had been on first
Arriving and drove slowly toward East Dean;
Cautiously crawling home in the left lane
—A gambler's skill Americans *must* learn—
Topped a rise and saw, coursing blue terrain,
A cloud-shaped horse, in sunshot beauty burn—
Lady as mist and light, racing again.

THE CELTIC LILT

FOR KITTY NORRIS

I've forgotten what we talked of, we four,
That first evening in Sussex together,
Unaware we'd one day stroll a Maine shore
Or owl haunted paths through Scottish heather.
Bemused that night by Kitty's Welsh accents,
The Celtic lilt of English on her tongue,
I'm certain my replies made little sense
To words she spoke that seemed less said than sung.

If my responses then seemed out of joint,
If I seemed in an after-dinner daze,
My wits adrift, my jests beside the point,
Think of it, Kitty, as a form of praise.

For that first rudeness you must forgive me.
Your words caressed my ears too musically.

KING CANUTE'S DAUGHTER

1.

Where Bosham's lanes have seas to wash their feet,
The church, with old unblinking eyes, records
Another tide's advance and its retreat,
Nearly inured to time and tourist hordes.

Here, where the tides of sea and men are met,
Among the accumulations of creeds,
Men have petitioned their gods to abet
Their finest and their most dubious deeds.

Witness to Roman, Saxon, Norman grief,
Your stone and wood are saturate with pleas
Of king, fisherman, carpenter and thief
When, fortunes failed, they fell upon their knees.

No regal pomp, no panoplied intrigues,
None of the sunken power of the great,
Who drowned their souls to gain a few more leagues,
Alters the sway of tidal suck and spate;

Or moves me as much as your minute grave,
Daughter of Canute, dead beneath the floor
Of the church, like some small, aborted wave
Lost at sea before it could reach the shore.

Walking through the myth-encrusted mollusc,
An arched and girded, time-enthralling shell,
I pause to read in the hushed, sea-washed dusk
Your inscription, the little known to tell.

At its foot, stroked in careful, childish script,
The brief tale of the dead daughter is told;
And at its head, guarding this simplest crypt,
A child's painted raven reigns—black and bold.

2.

Canute, I'd not known you had a daughter.
A doubtful myth suggests the sea's water
In tidal spate was a sworn enemy
You'd sought vainly to stay. But monarchy,
As all man's powers, has bounds; that you knew.
Your lost daughter had so instructed you,
When she, borne on death's swift, receding sea
Drifted away, while you watched helplessly,
Aware no sovereign ever could forestall
Or alter death's or the sea's rise and fall.
Where tides encroached, your court all gathered round,
You affirmed neither could be quenched or bound.

3.

Accept, accept, accept Canute;
The scouring waves will wash away
As much as towering waves will give.
Never too young to die or live,
We cannot hasten, cannot stay
Them. Accept Canute and be mute.

4.

Leaving the sea-rapt, dozing church I spied,
Hung from the front seat of a motor car,
An infant, suspended in a cocoon
Of white, the warm, soft rhythms of its sleep
Barely heard; then thought I sensed a faint sigh,
As when sand-absorbed wavelets seethe and die,
And fancied this babe, sprung from the human deep,
Was some foam-furred seafruit a summer moon
Mistook for the strayed daughter's avatar,
And coaxed gently landward on a warm tide.

5.

An unlikely thought and yet it might be,
Since we landlings, offsprung from Mother Sea,
Are her forked, upright, finless progeny
And testify with salty blood and tears
To those lost, ancestral, aquatic years.
Those daughters *could* be sisters it appears.

THE SMALLEST DAISIES

FOR CHRISTOPHER FRY

Farthings strewn by a careless lord,
Indifferent to their little worth,
The stemless daisies cling to earth
In random patterns on the sward.

Bright blemishes, they mar the true,
The impeccable, stainless sheen
Of close-shorn, lustrous, speckless green
As saturate and total hue.

So too stars in their steepest height
Of blueness nearly absolute
With spattered flickerings dilute
The deepest blue with flecks of light.

Though daisies, steadfast in the grass,
Immune to loftiest desire,
Know man and stars, rising higher,
Have, too, their seasons and will pass.

Resistless, they'll not be denied
By any trimly mowing man,
Until they've had their season's span,
Passing when they alone decide.

So small, so close to earth they lean,
You doubt they ever could survive,
Yet there they are and still alive
After the whirling guillotine

Of mower blades decapitates
Ambitious crowds of fleshy grass,
Surviving every shearing pass,
Which scarcely one eradicates.

They scoff at him who seeks a lawn
Of thick, unblemished, cherished green,
With not one daisy to be seen.
They mock his ban; they won't be gone.

Each cleaving to its lowly place,
Without pretence they yet persist
By soft refusal to resist,
Turning sunward a sun's small face.

They don't agree that they're a weed.
Wisely refusing to contend,
They know that surely in the end
The lovers of lawns must concede

That a daisied green greener gleams,
As any theory, incomplete,
Is nearer truth than one so neat
It quite excludes untidy dreams.

The frustrate mower, glancing back,
Beholds a trail of daisy discs,
Small, stubborn escapees from risks,
Lighting his and his mower's track.

Rueful, he grins, now self-amused;
Poets, he grants, should, more than most,
Know that truth's a volatile host
Of paradoxes, loosely fused.

Swaying wraiths from his pipe attest
At all times it should be assumed,
Smoke, truth and lawns may seem too groomed;
Order being chaos at rest;

A living rest which can evoke
Out of what is that which may be,
Through an intricate repartee
Among substance, seeming and smoke.

He had hoped this monotonous,
Peaceful, pacing occupation
Might provide no provocation
Or any sort of stimulus;

No tragic tears, no comic joys,
No grapplings with rich disorders,
Walking tightrope on thin borders,
In dialogs of transient poise.

Daisies held with no wordy strife;
Theirs was forthright philosophy:
Being proving its right to be
By being, verifying life.

Who was he to discriminate?
No poet was a proxy God,
Even to peasants of the sod.
Who *should* decide a daisy's fate?

Keyless he hums, then starts to sing
Excerpts from music uncomposed;
Themes no one had yet supposed,
In the strange key of everything.

One thing for sure he knew he knew:
No pure green could ever compare
To flowered green, no void night air
To impure splendors of starred blue.

THE WREN

FOR PHYLLIS FRY

"The smallest, warm, brown bird of the region,
Troglodytes, troglodytes" say books
That classify and list the high legion
Of the sky-skimmers, their songs, their homes, their looks.

Webster, consulted on the last two words,
Says, "an unsocial, reclusive person"
Is a troglodyte. But why among birds
So brand the wren? No chapter and verse on

Her says less. Minute mite of earth turned air,
As vibrant as a mandolin's twanged string,
Unobserved observer of each affair,
She, from her hidden post—missing no thing—

Bobs then her perked up tail and flips a trill,
In a commentary as light and keen
As a sun-shaft that picks out on a hill
Some small green revelation none had seen.

HEROES

For those anonymous Londoners who endured the
blitzing of their homes and city
with grace and courage

Spare me, please, the mood Napoleonic.
Those pouter-pigeon types, strutting in stride
To music heroically moronic,
Are brass without, papier-mâché inside.

Give me modest heroes who storm each day
As though they just might possibly come through
Unwounded—though statistics lie in wait—
Coolly collaborating with a fate
Much too bleak to dwell on. Give them their due,
Those unsung soldiers who shun all display;

Who, when worlds founder and fountains go dry,
When homely lintels break and dark birds cry,
Muster up, through lips cracked by bitter brew,
Some assorted jests and a song or two.

THE CHOIR SINGS PURCELL

To church we'd clumped, both gumboot shod,
Trudging through night-rain, mud and sludge,
Put out with the weather and God;
Yet slowly yielding to the spell
Of the clear voices and Purcell,
Felt shame to think we might begrudge

An act of belief where such notes,
Floating in hallowed space, as light
As sunlit throngs of weightless motes,
With faith's bright melodies defied
The melancholy skies outside,
When children sang Purcell that night.

And knew we'd never hear so well
As in this nearly artless church,
Such pure, young voices lift Purcell,
In mingled octaves rising higher,
As though some birds had trained this choir
In how to reach the highest perch.

Echoed in music, we went out
Into a night where rain still fell
Upon both skeptic and devout,
Just as the seeping, sodden sky
Parted to show one star swim by;
A high, bright truant from Purcell.

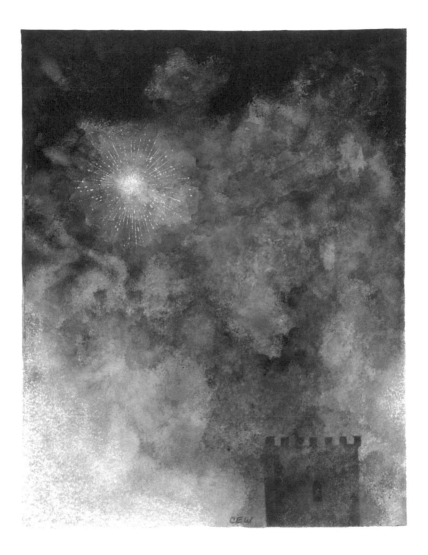

SOME BROODINGS AT BIGNOR

With the Roman dominion done
Beneath the bashful Anglish sun,
The Caesars gone from land they'd seized,
Some things were lost among those won.

When the subduing, taloned tread
Of legions with an eagle's head
—Unappeasable, unappeased—
Were only a remembered dread;

Bandied about where old men talk
Of past heroics as they walk
Through twilights of themselves and day
Past villas sunk to mother chalk;

Most things gone no one could regret.
Law and order may still the fret
And fray that's the anarchic way
Of life. Rome ruled well. Yet forget

Never—what's ordered is the point!
Rome, always eager to annoint
And to emulate all things Greek,
Wrenched the Greek spirit out of joint.

Here, where some shreds of Rome remain,
Where silent shards and tools explain,
The marred mosaic figures speak
Less of things holy than profane.

What Rome failed most to understand
Is that you must not shut your hand
And make the bird a pinioned prize
After persuading it to land.

The Roman itch was to name it,
To close the mailed fist and claim it,
To classify and organize,
Though, so doing, they might maim it.

Hurled like lances, Rome's highways flew,
Their stone-shod courses piercing through
Bogs and barriers, cold and fire,
To lands of Angle, Frank and Jew,

Carrying systems, edicts, goads,
The fasces of coercive modes,
To bind gross grandeurs of empire.
Some rare things shunned all laws and codes.

I, a man with not much pretence
To scholarship, instead a sense
That definition is a snare,
That life eludes in self-defense

The tidy bureaucratic mind,
The too constrained and well-defined,
Must make some effort to be fair.
I'd not have Rome too much maligned.

Let's credit Rome with something warm
To moderate the sunless norm
Of Sussex's sullen winter damp
And soften rigors of "good form."

Though here "good form" does not displace
Informal goodness or that grace
Which in the castle or the camp
Gentles the frigid home or face.

I would testify, for my part,
That "central heating" from the heart,
Fueled by a cup or two of tea,
Is not an unknown English art.

Yet, when the chill invades my spine,
Breaching warm moats of tea or wine,
I think of Rome regretfully
And a hypocaust becomes a shrine;

A shrine to no high deity,
Nor one Roman exclusively.
Americans agree with them
That heating's best done centrally.

Most things Roman were better lost,
Though who could estimate the cost,
Who sang a modest requiem
When Britain lost the hypocaust?

Hypocaust: an ancient Roman central-heating system.

A SEMI-DETACHED ODE

TO CERTAIN B.B.C. COMMENTATORS

Oh, those careful, cultivated voices,
Queasy, all, at any ill-bred noises,
Terribly cultured, painfully refined,
Their standards absolute and well-defined,
Surveying art from their high pinnacle,
Hygienic, distant and clinical,
In tones sad, reproachful and omniscient,
Suggest every master was deficient.
Less than charitable in inspection,
Theirs is the sharpest sort of dissection,
Unalloyed by any careless spasm
Of crass and off-guard enthusiasm.

Sniffing through noses skilled in detection
Of the faintest whiff of imperfection,
They accuse the artist of not doing that
He did not set out to do. Caveat
And objections are the dry crops they reap;
The grounded flight and the miscarried leap.
They grant no defective art its small meed
Of praise, though it may meet some human need.
Rarely do I hear one of them suggest
When their own definition of the "best"
Has not been met, "Perfection, on most counts,
May serve man best in limited amounts."

Or remark of those who joust and tourney
With themselves on art's perplexing journey,
Whose lodestars, unreliable as chance,
Point toward no ends any know in advance,
"It is as much the making as the made
Which can render us solace, light and aid."
The keenest scalpel of critical mind,
Which would lay bare both art and life may find
Secrecies recede, finalities fade,
For life's a quick ghost which will not be laid.
Eluding glib morticians of the arts,
Blood no longer flows from post-mortemed hearts.

SNOWDROPS

Why are poetry's Pooh-Bahs so averse
To what they heavily ban as "light verse"?
The farthest outskirts of the universe,
I've been told, can be reached only by "light."

I'd hesitate to style something minor
When I know the subtlest designer,
Playing against the major the minor,
Opens with minor keys a major height.
"Light," it seems, is not quite the same as "slight."

Today, a brave and small minority,
The year's first snowdrops, tracing warmer white
Against backward Spring's latest drop of snow,
Bloomed in a nearby dooryard under skies
Which suggested their venture was unwise.
Their heads bent under the late winter's blow,
Somehow they had turned the heavy scene "light,"
Unaware they were minor poetry.

LESS IS MORE

Less is more. . . . I confess
I agree with that—more or less.
Nature is nothing, if not dutiful
To all the hard demands
Of need. The ultimate command's
Survival. The beautiful
Is what's left over, some whim
Within severity.

A liquid tree
Reflected where fishes swim,
A weightless reflection
Shivered on the water's skin,
Is useless, unless to panicked fin,
Wary of detection.

Who can doubt that necessity, bare,
Carries the greatest force?
Whether we do or don't endorse
Its ultimatums, they are there,
And yet. . . . No birds that haste
The morning into light,
Helping it shrug off the night,
Count a few extra notes as waste.

Winter here in Sussex is a sometime thing.
Yesterday, walking out into a false Spring,
Birds I hadn't known were there began to sing.
Following a score they were born and bred to,
They sang their prescribed melodies through and through,
And some few notes more than they strictly had to.

CHRIST IN PICCADILLY CIRCUS —
GOOD FRIDAY

The trumpets blat and shiny slide-trombones
Slither through traffic snarls glissando tones
And tubas, like Hercules breaking wind,
Or like deep-voiced reminders man has sinned,
Emphasize the evangelical beat
Of hymn-tunes and the rhythmic, marching feet . . .
And there, at the procession's head is one
Bearing the cross of today's anguished son.

And suddenly, in the brash, raunchy square,
The multitudes pause; a strange thing is there.
The friz-topped young in tattered dungarees,
Turbaned Sikhs, tourist freaks, civil Bobbies,
Glances stayed, for a moment hold their breath.
No single soul of them convinced that death
Can be overcome, they eye the borne cross,
Then turn, seeking anodynes against loss,

Toward shops devoted to the tricks of sex
And trade, the cinemas where Three-Gun Tex
Blasts his way through assorted villainies
Near a columned Eros aiming to please.
The blue-serged Salvationists pass along,
Their hymns displaced by the dissonant song
Of traffic squeals rising through diesel fumes,
As the heedless, numbing, frenzied flow resumes.

All things considered, Christ, it's surely best
Your final agonies were not staged here.
You might well have been subject to arrest.
Traffic must move; the streets must be kept clear.

POPPIES — SUSSEX AND SIENA

Many who've held that blood is wine,
Have also held that flesh is bread,
And, thinking on both, I'd incline
To agree with much they've said,
When, up the downs and down through folds,
The Sussex poppies torch the wheat,
Smelting the greens toward harvest golds
Of bread's condensed, sustaining heat.

When, in my mind's eye, I return
To the Sienese vineyards, where,
Like floral tinder poppies burn,
Nearly kindling the summer air,
I know then wine is liquid fire,
And that same liquid fire is blood,
And all of living things a pyre,
Set aflame by its scarlet flood.

Fragile arsonists, poppies light
Sussex downs and Sienese knolls;
Their brief and scattered brands ignite
A burning text on rolling scrolls,
Proclaiming there for all to see,
That bread and wine are kindred forms
Of that one flame we seek and flee
From, which consumes us as it warms.

DONS AND SWANS

Much preoccupied with "Higher Things,"
The Dons punt the Cam's meanderings.
Immune to Nature's close distractions,
They pursue loftier abstractions—
"The True Nature Of Truth," possibly—
And in search of that may fail to see
"The True Truth Of Nature" around them,
A diversion which might astound them,
Which might dilute the purity they
Seek where lazy currents purl and play.

Lost in mazed, philosophical themes,
More twisting than alluvial streams,
They may, despite opened eyes, be blind
To all but counterfeit birds the mind
Contrives, and miss the swans. Galleons
In full sail, whiter than novice nuns
And fiercer, they glide by. Theories
Are colder than they, whose grace wearies
Us less than the most recondite thought
The rarest of scholars ever taught.

It would be no cause for alarm,
Or do permanent harm,
If, every now and then, the Dons
Looked up and saw the swans.

A CHANCE MEETING IN A PUB

"I'm a simple man," he declared,
Flashing a frank and winsome smile,
Which seemed entirely free of guile,
As I, struck speechless, gulped and stared,
Incredulous and astounded,
Wondering if he really knew
Himself—or anyone else who
Held a belief that unfounded;
Since a "simple man" is at least
As rare as any Unicorn
Or Roc and is as seldom born
As either legendary beast.

But if he chose to, who was I
To challenge his unlikely claim,
Or disabuse him in the name
Of honesty or testify
His simplicity was a ruse?
Intent as all who live and thrive
By masquerade, he'd too survive
By devices they'd come to use.
The insect that's in rest a stick;
The flounder shamming ocean floor;
The butterfly that's one bloom more;
Persist by an instinctive trick.

All, on metamorphosis bent,
By being what they cannot be
Disarm the world; both they and we
Wear artifice as armament.

Then he, who wore a simple mask
To gull the world, lifted his brew.
"This amber cheer," he said, "will do
To answer all I care to ask."

REVOLUTIONARY REFLECTIONS ON
THE VILLAGE GREEN

1.

One spring day, strolling on the village green,
In easy chat of cabbages and kings,
Our talk veered suddenly toward violent things,
Toward revolutions past and those forseen.
"You know," he said, "I've always borne in mind,
When the revolutionary fires burn,
A revolution is one complete turn;
And when the wheel has come to rest you'll find
Things as they were except for those who lost
Their lives beneath the turning wheel, their cost
As immeasurable as it is blind.
Even when they seem called for, I'm averse
To revolutions, since I've noticed these,
Once won, are prone to go from bad to worse,
When they're run by revolutionaries.

Since life offers no better solutions
I'd favor love's daily revolutions."

2.

When judged by what I've seen and see,
His measured words seemed truth to me.
Much as I respect invention,
Still and all I count it no sin
To see the new as what it's been.
A revolution's intention
May merely revise convention.
I'm wary of the deadly din
Of witless nitroglycerin,
Which can lose more than it has won,
Since it indiscriminately
May slay both bomber and bombee.

3.

Crocuses bloomed beneath a budding tree.
We headed toward The Toft to have some tea.

A ROMEO AND JULIET

Act 6 and perhaps Act 7

Will, as usual, you knew just when to stop,
To call a halt, to let the curtain drop.
The star-crossed victims of a prankish fate,
Both dead because a message came too late,
You leave abandoned there within the tomb,
Their death illuminating mortal gloom;
In that brief prelude to worms forever young,
Not by marriage or mortgages unstrung.
Your artistry quite unblemished, no touch
Of daily mar or wear's allowed to smutch
The shining tragedy of love broken
Before it had become a threadbare token
Both partners had lost or somehow mislaid
In a drawer they'd one day marked—Bills-Unpaid—.

You knew better than to write one more act
Or two—your art rounded, complete, compact.
But they, Will, both so young, did you ask them
If they craved your premature requiem—
Those deaths with which you crowned your knowing art?
Did each play willingly the assigned part?
Trapped between art and life, given a choice,
They might have answered with a single voice,
"We, who have seen our noble sires caught
Between the lives they led and those they ought,
And watched our mothers try to stay with paint
The encroachments of time's withering taint,
Would still, if it is all the same to you,
Prefer to live, to see the whole thing through."

I ask this, Will, though you'd no doubt reply,
"These are but creatures of my inner eye,
Imaginings, immune to death or pain,
Who live only on stage to entertain
An audience, those refugees from life,
Who allay with a simulated strife
That all too real reality that hounds
Them. Then too, I had need of pence and pounds.
Art I sought, but also sweet prosperity;
Who can submit his bills to posterity
And have any assurance they'll be paid?"
Shrugging, he might add, "A youth and maid,
Racked by family feuds and their smitten hearts,
Provide a sure-fire plot with two fat parts.

Hard on the heels of love, domestic bliss
Or cozy boredom could only dull this
Multicolored tale of love's persistence
Over time and time's bloodless insistence
That all becomes pallid, all fades away,
Even love, in the blanching light of day.
When both the poetry and the moon sink,
It's nearly impossible, I would think,
To make high drama out of married cares;
Like funding for their palazzo's repairs,
Doubts about where in summer they would go,
Given the rents for villas on the Po,
Their carking concerns as, passions cooling,
Love signified less than children's schooling."

You're right, Will, you knew what you were about.
Act Six we can easily do without,
As we can Act Seven, in which a scene
Staged above the piazza's travertine,
In a balcony, might painfully recall
Young lovers entwined in your words; in thrall
To their splendor, steeped in a lunar glow,
Reminders of things they'd sooner not know
Had been, in view of what they had become—
Two eunuch-ancients, old, spent, nearly numb.
Still, they might have traded that golden perch
For that rusty one where now they lurch
Slowly toward padded chairs to scan below
The daily traffic's bustling vertigo.

Though persuaded first-love's conflagration
Age may cool to ashen irritation,
They might, despite that, have wished one more act
Or two, which your play's art knowingly lacked.
Old now past hoping, arthritic fingers,
Should they touch, might stir a ghost that lingers
Into life, that fumbling warmth might revive
A past neither one knew was still alive;
And what had been, is, and what still might be,
Be all co-existent reality.
They might, now as then, choose not art but breath,
Saying, "Each breath is one breath less of death."
It might be so, Will, yes it might be so;
And neither of us, Will, will ever know.

MORE THAN MOST

FOR ANDREW YOUNG

Ungarrulous as flint,
Sparing of the too-rich word,
He—devotee of hint,
Recorder of flower, bird,

Sky, down, grass, dung-heap, mole—
Saw each particle and trace
As singular and whole
And uniquely commonplace.

Most provident of bards,
He saved what man overlooks,
As twigs the tree discards
Live twice in the nest of rooks.

What we in passing by
Never saw or seeing lost
He rescued for our eye
At the smallest verbal cost.

More than most, he knew
How very nearly nothing
Brought to closest view,
Can be nearly everything.

This he chose to sing.

Charles E. Wadsworth, a painter and printmaker who has spent many years on an island off the Maine coast, has illustrated *Root And Sky* and *Death Is A Kind of Love*, both by Christopher Fry; *Andrew Young — Remembrance And Homage*, a memorial tribute to an Anglo-Scottish poet; *Seed Leaves* by Richard Wilbur; *The Long Sought Landscape* by Charles Seymour Alden; *Islands Off Maine* by Leslie Norris; *Fireweed and Other Poems* by William H. Matchett; and a selection of his own poetry called *Views From The Island*.

600
copies of
this book have
been printed at
The Stinehour Press
on Mohawk Superfine Text
in Monotype Bell.
Freeman Keith
designed
it.

The
watercolors
were reproduced
photo-offset
by Meriden
Gravure.

ಌ